ALL THESE TREES

TOM EARLEY

Gomer Press
1992

First Impression—1992

ISBN 086383 866 9

© Tom Earley

Printed by J. D. Lewis & Sons Ltd.,
Gomer Press, Llandysul, Dyfed, Wales.

To Elizabeth

Acknowledgements

Some of these poems originally appeared in *Outposts, Poetry Wales, Tribune, Anglo-Welsh Review, Planet, Welsh Nation, Arcade* and *London Welshman.*

Some appeared in the following anthologies: *Voices of Today* (John Murray, 1980) *London Lines* (Methuen, 1982) *Anglo-Welsh Poetry, 1480 to 1980* (Poetry Wales Press, 1984) *The Valleys* (Poetry Wales Press, 1984) and *A Book of Wales* (Dent, 1987).

A number were read and discussed on *Radio Wales* (Anita Morgan's Programme), *Radio 4* (Poetry Please), *Radio 3* (Poetry Now) *Schools Radio (Wales), Schools Radio (Radio 4)* and the South-East Wales Arts Association Dial a Poem service.

What they said about *Rebel's Progress* (Gomer, 1979)

'*Rebel's Progress* is Tom Earley's third book and by far his best. His virtues are predominantly: clarity, vividness, humour, wit and form.'

[Derek Stanford, *Books and Bookmen*]

'*Rebel's Progress* is in the main stream of Welsh radicalism, socialist and pacifist. Tom Earley is one of the lineage of Idris Davies and Gwyn Thomas and he takes his place there as of right.'

[Sally Roberts Jones, *Book News*]

'Tom Earley is another whose work I have enjoyed. The best poems in this new volume are again those arising from recollections of Welsh life and landscape.'

[Norman Nicholson, *Church Times*]

'Here there is a poet's respect for words, for the rhythm of heightened speech.'

[Colin Palfrey, *Welsh Nation*]

'Quiet appraisal of natural things in an idiom consciously poetic with a neatness of form and lack of irony which echoes both Edward Thomas and Dylan Thomas.'

[Julian A. Dutton, *Outposts*]

'Effective, controlled accounts which gain warmth and immediacy from their strong narrative line, dramatic voice and simple language.'
[Andrew Clark, *Poetry Wales*]

'Far and away the best feature of these poems is their Welsh musicality. He has a perfect ear for the Welsh voice and a felicity in relating its natural rhythms to the rhythms of verse.'
[Margaret Melicharova, *The Pacifist*]

'He is a predominantly celebratory poet. A poet who feels and describes rather than one who thinks and analyses.'
[Richard Poole, *Anglo-Welsh Review*]

'Bloomsbury and its views from a flat provide, in poetic terms, nothing as striking as the cadences of Welsh English, so beautifully captured in one or two poems here.'
[Lawrence Sail, *Stand*]

'The valley poems, words wrapped round the village, the colliery, the choir and the mountains, gently ooze *hiraeth*.'
[Dafydd Nicholas, *London Welshman*]

'Good though the poems about London, and even places abroad, are to read, it is the Welsh works which remain in the memory.'
[Rhiannon Williams, *The Leader*]

Contents

NEW POEMS

SELECTED POEMS

New Poems

Home for St. David's Day

Wales wrapped itself around me
Like a warm Llandysul shawl.
Cardiff had colour, miscellany
Of crocuses in Cathays Park
And the first daffodils for David.
But the journey up the valley was grey
And here in the shadow of the hills
The woods are dark above the sombre town.

No leaves, even on the larch, nothing,
Nothing but strings of black beads
Against the sky, no light except
From hazel catkins glowing in the gloom
Dangling like insecure caterpillars;
And clustered lamps of coltsfoot on the path.
Not a single lamb yet in Gelli-ddu;
Only a little calf shut in a shed.

Because the pasture is poor,
The pregnant ewes are eating swedes
And tough fabricated food-blocks.
This is the peewits' pinch of Wales
But the mountain grass is gold,
The bracken copper, the distant beacons
Silver in the limpid evening light.
The shawl of Wales keeps me warm.

Yr Hen Iaith
'O bydded i'r hen iaith barhau'

I remember an ailanthus in Gwaelod y Garth,
A forest-tree so huge, it darkened
The windows of a third-floor flat
And had to be cut down, its trunk
Viciously sliced by a screaming saw
Until it was level with the ground.
Two years later, some twenty young trees
Were growing in a circle from its stump.

I remember the quarry above Llety Siencyn,
Sheer cliff face and, single in the centre,
A silver birch growing from the bare rock.
Where is its earth? On what does it feed?
It looks as though it forced its way
Out of the solid stone, its powerful thrust
Creating the crack. Now its yellow leaves
Are shaking and shining in the autumn sun.

I remember childhood's coal-tip, in Caegarw,
Insulting black against the hillside's green;
But now the woods have spread around its flanks,
Bluebells in May and violets by the stream.
The summit is velveted with moss; harebells
Among its summer grasses, foxgloves, fern.
Only the soil is coloured by the coal.
The tip's become the mountainside again.

The Apple
(from the Welsh of Euros Bowen)

It was night,
like night before the existence of Adam,
in a world without form and void,
and only the moon
in the centre of mist on every side
stirring in the sight.

And here the mist was
the stillness of a lake
and the moon's form now
like blossoms of an apple tree shimmering
in the midst of the water.

Surprised eyes lighted
there
on the strange garden
and imagination began to move
soft footed
in the light.

Then stooping,
like curious Adam,
to gather up the dust—
four thousand million years
of dust
there
an apple
now
in the palm of a hand.

Anglo-Welsh Entitlement

Turning away from the forgotten country,
Escaping at last from the night's prison,
He began to climb the sad mountain
In the direction of snipe's castle,
Hoping to reach the inns of love.

Yesterday in the heat of the sun,
He had loitered across the burning sand
In Barry Island; then turning his back
On funland and circus, had decided, with a small
Desperation, to take the diesel to yesterday,
Up the winding valley to see his mother
And sisters, cherished tenants of the house.

Not that he brought flowers, not
Even ransoms, though he knew
Where they grew, skilled as he was
At finding gold in the woods,
Not only plants but animals and birds.
He had always known the mountains
Polecats pheasants still inhabited,
Exiles all, in the green desert.

The line of knowledge went a long
Way back; even the stones remember.
The boy inside recalled it all,
Not with a sense of time, but with
A sense of something far more vague.
The changing shadow of a certain tree
Became the sundial for his days.

He remembered the bitter spell
Of winter weather with the snow
On the mountain, snow everywhere,
Covering all the tips, blocking roads,
Snow, the mask of pity,
Hiding the ugly features of the town.

And then came the thaw,
Twentieth-century flood, the water
Pouring off the trees like green rain.
The ffrwd was a mountain torrent
Crashing over the blue bed of the blue
Pennant quarry, definition of a waterfall.
He heard the water music all around.

Each visit to his valley home
Contained both requiem and celebration.
He did not come for ancestor worship,
Being far more often aware
Of the loss of ancestry.

The province of belief was his chief
Concern, but to the socialist within him
Nationalism sometimes seemed parochial.
As well as a love of Wales, perhaps
One needed to have a sense of Europe.
H'm.

Deep Dyffryn is dead

Deep Dyffryn is dark now; but then
When we were young, the pit-head yard was bright,
The light-filled lamp-room sparkled on the night.
Reluctant groups of night-shift men
Collected lamps while loitering toward the cage,
(Each man a star, a disembodied light)
Resplendent ballet on a blacked-out stage.

Deep Dyffryn is silent now; but then
We lived inside the noises from the yard.
Throughout the morning-shift we heard
Men's voices call above the background din
Of sawmill's whining, anvil's clang,
Clatter of dram, rattle of horse's chain
And humming of the winding-engine's song.

Deep Dyffryn is dead now; its chill
Yard, which ghosts of miners haunt,
Deserted, sinister and grim.
All that remains are two gaunt
Wheels, that cut the line of hill,
The pit-head gear already out of trim,
Its winding-engine permanently still.

Another Winter (Englyn)

The last withered leaves are lying, the wind
Begins its bleak crying
And the blackbird does not sing.
Even *his* love is dying.

The Soup Kitchen
(a memory of 1926)

Are you letting it get cold?
Start it, there's a good boy.

Don't you like this lovely soup?
Try just a small spoonful.

Shall I make you a sandwich?
At least we've got some cheese.

Why don't you say something, lad?
It's rude not to answer.

Are you feeling ill or what?
Your face is thin and pale.

Why are you crying, my dear?
Please tell me what is wrong.

*'Our mam is at 'ome by 'erself
And she 'avent got nothing to eat.'*

All we like Sheep

The only floral tribute taken
To the cemetery was the family-wreath.
Jones the Flowers had done a marvellous job
And the result was a work of art.
The heart-shaped part of the wreath
Consisted of white chrysanthemums
And across it was the name, Emrys,
In red roses, thirty seven in all.

The service ended at half past two.
When the mourners left the cemetery,
This beautiful wreath, which cost twenty pounds,
Was lying on an adjoining grave.
At ten to three, a few relations
Of the dead man decided to visit
The grave and found that the wreath
Had already been utterly devoured by sheep.

The family blamed the council
For not maintaining the fences and gates.
It's disgusting, they said, that flowers
Left on graves, are allowed to suffer
In this way from the depredations of sheep.
It was bad enough that funeral cars
Had to slow down to a stop to wait
For wandering sheep to get out of the way.

One of the mourners who returned
Said, 'I was speechless, very upset
And annoyed when I discovered
That, within eighty minutes of the funeral,
Only the wire frame of the wreath
And some messy bits of moss were left.
It is just not good enough
And what would Emrys have said?'

Brachi's

We patronised Franchi and Conti,
Fulgoni, Sterlini, Ferrari,
But called every café a brachi
Because of the Bracchis of Bardi.

On desolate nights of the winter
We went in for comfort and shelter,
Hot coffee and pies from the steamer,
Because of the Bracchis of Bardi.

We flirted with Clara and Gina,
Maria, Silvana and Pina
And chatted with Bruna and Dina
Because of the Bracchis of Bardi.

Made friends with Luigi and Dario,
Romano, Pierino and Tonio,
Giuseppe, Enrico and Mario
Because of the Bracchis of Bardi.

On luminous nights of the summer
We sat with an iced sarsparilla,
Discussing the next season's rugger,
Because of the Bracchis of Bardi.

We patronised Franchi and Conti,
Fulgoni, Sterlini, Ferrari,
But called every café a brachi
Because of the Bracchis of Bardi.

Craig y Dyffryn Revisited

Sycamore, ash and silver birch,
Their roots completely burnt away,
Lie with their arms out on the coaly soil
Like colliers overcome by gas, or caught
By fire from explosion underground.
Trees that still stand are blackened skeletons,
Each trunk propped up by crippled neighbour,
Remaining branches charred disfigured stumps.

This tip above a wood is burning now.
Dormant for years while deep down inside
Small coal and gas combined in slow combustion;
At last it has erupted, summit smouldering,
Fern, grass and fallen twig changing to charcoal.
Here smoke is forcing out through narrow cracks,
There angry flames spurt and recede, leaving
Red hot embers of waste coal and wood.

And yet the woods below appear to be
Inviolable in their summer peace.
Beyond those trees untouched so far by fire
There is a clearing bounded by a crowd
Of pink and purple foxgloves tall as men
While in their midst, and tightly packed as though
They had been planted purposively there,
A deeper purple mass of willow herb.

Not nicknamed fireweed for fun, this ardent flower
Will choose to grow on ground that has been burnt.
When war had stopped, it seemed to come at once
And cover every ugly bombed-out site,
Completely hiding all the violence.
Here too, if all these trees should be destroyed,
The willow herb would fill the space, the woods
Become a home for butterflies and bees.

The Shepherd of Kares
(from the Welsh of Euros Bowen)

The village of Kares breeds shepherds,
herdsmen of sheep and goats,
in the shadow of Neapolis in the island of Crete.

It did so in the years
of Owain Glyn Dŵr's care,
when Petros Philarges left
the hillsides there
around distant Neapolis
for the fields of Oxford and Paris
and became keeper of the fold in Milan,
when the Great Schism tore
at the hedges of the habitations of the Faith.

But under the wisdom of his crook
he rose to become
head-shepherd of Christendom,
the lad from the village of Kares in Crete
a lord in Rome,
when Owain Glyn Dŵr,
in days rent asunder,
was an outlawed hand in the habitation
of the sheep and goats
of his own charge in Wales.

All these Trees are Mine

Oy-oy walked through the Dyffryn woods
In a bowler hat and navy blue suit.
Sometimes he stood quite still on the path
And stared through his gold-rimmed glasses
At the glistening sky, smiling with satisfaction
To see it so beautiful. Often he talked
To the gorsedd stones, laughing at their replies.
Suddenly he would wave his arms about
And shout, 'All these trees are mine'.
Then, having thus released his libido,
He would start for home relaxed and refreshed.

But we were reluctant to let him go.
Jealous boys resenting his pleasure
We hid behind trees and teased,
'Oy-oy, Oy-oy, all these trees are mine,'
Followed him at a distance, throwing acorns
And conkers, 'All these trees are mine.'
But it was a disappointing game for he never
Gave us the satisfaction of chasing us.
Instead he hurried home, dignified, aloof.
Since then I've heard he was a minor bard
Winning chairs at local eisteddfodau.

And now it's my turn to be thought a little mad.
I roam the mountain like some latter day Oy-oy,
Shouting questions at the sheep and laughing
At their clever monosyllabic answers,
Leaping like schoolboy needlessly over brooks,
Calling names through the dry stone walls,
Mad too in my concern not to squash the fruit

On the bantam wimberry bushes, not to trample
The tiny yellow tormentil, and knowing
Their habitat, not to destroy grasshoppers,
Not to kill ants with my clod-hopping shoes.

Spring in Wales

It was Sunday morning,
A sunny day in late March,
And dad was free to take
His young daughters for a walk.
Let's go up through the larch
Woods to Gelliddu farm and look
At the little new-born lambs.

One lamb was crying piteously
Because it had lost its mother
But most were in merry mood
Racing and chasing across the field.
The children said that some
Were playing Follow My Leader
And some were playing Tag.

No one wanted to leave the farm
But suddenly dad realised they must
Hurry home for Sunday lunch.
They got there with time to spare
And with healthy appetites.
What have we got to eat, mam?
Your favourite dinner, love: lamb

The World Tree

Frost yesterday, flurries of snow today
And a boisterous wind from the north
Work the trees into a frenzy,
Shaking the trunks, making the twigs
Shiver and the leafless branches writhe.
Yet at this moment out there in the cold,
Three birds are on their nests laying eggs
In time for the family feast of Seder,
For the Passover, for Easter.

The pigeon clings to her precarious perch
On the swaying plane tree, breasts the branch,
Moving with it, rocking with it,
The celtic tree, the thing in between,
Joining earth and heaven, the celtic cross.
Reproduction, renewal, rebirth, resurrection.
After the winter of Lent, tomorrow's
Spring; after holy Saturday's darkness,
The light of Easter Day.

Do not decorate the church
With sentimental flowers.
Bring to the green man: twigs
Of the mystic oak, sprays of mysterious ash.
Adorn the pillars, the gothic stone trees,
With buds of sacred ash and druid oak.
Let the in-between things
Break into green, like the new grass
On the churchyard graves.

Seal Culling

(For Ross Gilligan, whose first-hand account inspired the poem)

From the helicopter high above the sea,
Strands of red wool appeared to stretch
Across the ice; descending, we realised
That they were yard-wide streams of blood
Dispersing from a pile of white pelts
Cut with sharp knives from dead seals
And stacked up neatly on the ice floe.

When we reached the place, we saw
Untidy heaps of carcases, hundreds
Of them, and blood, blood everywhere.
Ordinary men and unremarkable teenagers
Were clubbing young seals to death.
Clothes, hands, faces of the hunters
Were spattered with wet strips of flesh.

A baby seal, trying desperately to escape,
Fell into a narrow stretch of deep water.
The seal pup's frightened cries only stopped
For moments when it swallowed mouthfuls.
It struggled to grip with its flippers
And managed to drag its little body
Wearily up on to the ice floe again.

One vicious knock from a baseball bat
Failed to stop its crying; the young man
Lit a cigarette with blood-stained fingers.
He raised his long thick club again
And brought it down on the pup's
Head with a nauseating thud.
Another heavy blow and the seal was dead.

Misunderstanding

They had the look of lovers
Who'd spent the night together.

Reluctantly they parted
To go their working ways.

She walked and turned to wave.
He went on unaware.

He walked and turned to wave.
She went on unaware.

Now each of them thinks
The other one loves less.

Vicious Circle

'Ive had to take a second job
To help pay for my car,
An evening office-cleaning job.
It's dear to run a car.'

I asked, 'Why not give up the car?'
She answered with a frown,
'Oh no, I need to have the car.
The new job's out of town.'

Soliciting

She wanted to look her best.
Her hair had been newly washed
With just a touch of blonde rinse.
Dressed in a shapely sweater
And her bottom-hugging jeans,
She cut a provocative figure
Standing on the corner in the sun.
But how did one begin?
She had never done this before.

When her first shyness wore off
She proved an enormous success,
Finding she liked what she did,
And was kept busy all day.
Was it beginner's luck or was she
More appealing than the others?
The trouble was that some men
Only stopped and chatted her up.
Perhaps they hadn't the cash.

By early evening she felt worn out.
A taxi-driver pulled up at the kerb,
'What time you packing it in, duck?
I'll run you home when you finish.'
He was young, spicy and dark.
She thought she could fancy him
And for a moment was tempted.
Then she remembered she had to take in
All the money and the unsold flags.

To Rosie on Burns Night

O, my Rose is like a red, red love
That fires me to the core.
O, my Rose is like the turtle-dove
That always asks for more.

So hot you are, my downy duck,
When in your bed we lie;
And I will love you still, with luck,
Till all the pubs go dry.

Till all the pubs run dry, my dear,
And fish-and-chip shops close,
O, I will love you never fear,
While you still want me, Rose.

I'd go through fire and water, dear,
To sleep with you again.
I'll come on Friday, if I'm near,
Though not if it should rain.

Mr. Eliot at the Swimming Pool

Autumn is the cruellest time, bringing
Regret for the dead holiday, changing
Patterns of living, substituting
Frugality for excess.
Summer kept us fit, covering
Skin in forgetful tan, putting
New life into old muscles.
Winter surprised us, coming to the baths
With no people, having the pool
To ourselves. I said, Rosie,
Rosie, hold me tight.
The attendant's not looking.
Oo, she said, oo, a wet cuddle.
Kinky. Very sexy, she said.
And down we went.
In the deep end, there you feel free.

As we came up, she seemed changed.
I forgot, no petting, she said, look
It says there on that poster:
No pushing, no ducking, no shouting,
No running, no wrestling, no petting.
But I saw only a heap of broken images:
The sea, the sea, the sand where the sun beats
And the cave under the red rock.
Ar lan y môr mae cerrig cochion,
Ar lan y môr mae lilis gwynion.
There is shadow under this red rock.
Come in under the shadow of this red rock.
Come on Rosie, no-one's looking,
And I will show you something different.

Examination at the Doom Door
(Ted Hughes, dreaming that he is on his death-bed in Tibet,
is catechized by the Dalai Lama.)

What was your attitude to pride?   *Enjoyed it.*
What was your attitude to wrath?   *Enjoyed it.*
What was your attitude to envy?   *Enjoyed it.*
Your attitude to lust?   *Enjoyed it.*
Your attitude to gluttony?   *Enjoyed it.*
To avarice?   *Enjoyed it.*
To sloth?   *Enjoyed it.*

To poetry, music and art?   *No*
                                          comment
Truth, beauty and goodness?   *No*
                                          comment.
To helping other people?   *No*
                                          comment.

I never did anyone any harm.   Ah.
Who shall I be in my reincarnation?   Crow.
Oh, no. Anything but that! Please.   Pass,
                                          Hughes.

The Sophisticated Blackbirds

March mornings saw them laying claim
To chosen territory in the square
And driving off persistent disputants.
The afternoons were still but as the light
Grew faint, the male began his aria unrehearsed
And, poor man's nightingale, continued
Con amore till after darkness fell.

The hen's unliberated role was played
In the snug centre of a laurel bush
So small that spikes of lilac thrust above,
Anticipating bright laburnum's chains.
The pink of ornamental may outlasted both
Until the pale syringa superseded it,
Dropping its petals on the truant young.

Their ragged nest, abandoned in July,
Revealed how inner city blackbirds build.
Worked in with customary weeds, mud, grass
Were bits of paper, string and cellophane,
Patches of silver foil, odd strips of polythene
And scarlet bristles from an office-cleaner's broom.
When will these birds discover sellotape?

Frustration

The pigeons sunbathed on the autumn lawn,
Collecting warmth against the coming cold.
Today their curious posture puzzled me:
Instead of their accustomed nestling down,
Squeezed in the grass as though they covered eggs,
They stood erect and still, facing one way,
Heads high on rigid necks.

Remaining quiet, I looked around
And saw behind the birds, alarmingly close,
A hunting cat poised for the kill.
His black body was pressed into the green
As flat as a plate. With ears down
And head lowered, he watched.
His mouth mimed inaudible cries.

He eased himself forward like a snake.
Now he was a yard from the nearest bird.
I held my breath. I did not see him spring,
Only heard the explosion of wings
And saw the massed flight, no hostage
Left, no victim. Like a swift scythe
The cat's angry tail slashed the turf.

Titmice

Comic blue-tit with black slanty eyes
And music-hall Chinaman's face,
You even have a whispering Chinese voice.
Tom Tit, Thumbelina, Tom Thumb,
Miniature acrobat, upside down
On the nut-cage at my window,
You still peep from behind
To see what I'm doing in my kitchen.
Is it safe, is it safe? you ask.

Handsome great-tit, you'd make
A sparkling colour-television picture.
Momentarily solemn in dramatic
Death-penalty judge's black cap
And scarf, you suddenly swoop,
More like the criminal, to grab.
Your flight's a flash of black
And white head, rainbow body,
Spanking, quirky navy-blue tail.

Grubby coal-tit, poor relation, shabby
Edition of the others with more
Sombre colours, I like you best
Of all; and once in Kew Gardens
You came out of the pines, straight
To my hand, as I held it out
Full of chopped nuts, tickling me
With your hairpin-thin legs
And frail spidery feet.

A Swan to her Cygnets

Remember, dears, the whole park
Will be intent on watching us.

Not a sound from one of you
As we glide along the lake.
There should be no need for me
To remind you not to behave
Like those plebeian ducklings,
Utterly undisciplined, wilfully disobedient
And such a worry to their harassed mother.

They dart off in so many directions,
She never knows which way to turn.
Try not to look at them, or pretend
You haven't seen, and treat them with contempt.
They are the scum of the pond
And, as you can imagine, they smell;
We must be thankful we aren't ducks.

Now children, into croc, single file please,
Allow a reasonable distance between you
And keep exactly behind each other.
One last word, my swan song,
Let us look proud to be swans.
Are you ready? Here we go.
Heads high, tails up, swim tall.

A Pair of Pigeons

Unlike the others, these two
Are uninterested in our food,
Intensely preoccupied, apart.

With little dancing steps
He sidles round her, hypnotizing.
Chauvinist, he puffs himself up,
Feels enormous, displays himself,
Thick neck and barrel chest.

Then a long bout of mutual
Grooming and vicious pecking
Of heads and necks; they seem
To enjoy even the most cruel jabs
As they move in mounting rhythm.

Suddenly she wants him,
Grabs his beak, locks
Him in a long kiss;
Deep throat, hold it, hold.
Then they break from the clinch.

She gets down for him now,
Makes herself small for him.
He climbs on top, treads her
Down lower and, with a great
Beating of wings, has finished.

They walk away from one another
Like strangers, satisfied, sober,
Searching again for food.

Blackbird in a Lime Tree

I stand here in Lincoln's Inn Fields
And note again how yellow leaves of lime
Contrast with its soot-coloured trunk
And how a fig-tree's slender arms
Support their shining shields of gold.
Foreign fruits of ailanthus, tree
Of heaven, burn yellow and red
Changing during sunshine into rust.
Plane-leaves litter colour on the lawn.

A blackbird alights on a lime
And at once becomes part of the tree,
His body-colour merging in a branch
And his beak matching yellow leaves.
Which is the darker black, his plumage
Or the boughs? Which is the brighter
Yellow, the foliage or his beak?
I savour making the choice and decide
The blackbird wins on both counts.

But why is he silent today?
Is this the bird that sang
Each morning in the Spring
And went on every evening after dark?
He does not sing now. I only hear
His panic calls. Of what is he afraid?
Only of the threatening frost? Or, like us,
Is he conscious he may never see
Another autumn's black and yellow lime?

Nocturnal Haiku

The star, that wanders
Out of its constellation,
Is an aeroplane.

Warnings

While you were out,
We called to service your fires.
Please phone us at the above address.
We shall be waiting to hear from you.

While you were out,
Love came but could not get in.
Useless to try for further contact.
You have thrown away your final chance.

While you were out,
We brought a parcel for you.
Please collect at the sorting office.
We shall need proof of identity.

While you were out,
God called but got no reply.
This has happened many times before.
Nothing you can do now, except wait.

Mors et Vita

I know that I am dead
Because I have never felt so cold.
Yet as I enter here, the place
Pleases me; everyone is naked
And there are beautiful women.
Free love, I think, eternal love.
All the girls I ever knew are here.

I look everywhere for my real love
Because I know she has arrived.
At last I find her; she comes to me
And I take her in my arms
But it only makes me feel more cold.
I try to speak but find I have no voice
Nor can I hear what she is trying to say.

I wonder with horror whether everyone
Here is deaf and dumb and desperately cold.
When I move my arms, she is gone.
I search endlessly but cannot find her.
The cold is becoming unbearable.
If only I could find my clothes again.
This can't go on for ever. It's absolute hell.

Halloween

As I stand, alone in the empty house,
Staring through my window at the full
Moon on this blustering autumn night,
A delicately graceful minuet dances out
From the radio behind me in the room.

The squally rain has stopped.
But raging winds are still
Fighting with the trees in the square
And thin clouds continue to drive
To the east, while the hunters' moon
Races west after its phantom game,
Now landlocked in clouds, now
Swinging free in a sea of navy blue.

Applause for la symphonie fantastique.
The streets are black and wet.
Coloured leaves cling to the pavement,
Stick into cracks between stones,
Build into banks against the gutters.

The concerto for two violins is now
Being played by Oistrakh and his son.
Doors bang and floor-boards creak
As invisible powers move through the house.
They have entered the room behind my back.
I feel their presence but I do not turn.
Why should I fear them—
The ghosts of Mozart, Berlioz and Bach?

Juxtaposition

As the late pigeons and last blackbirds
Disappear into the growing dark,
I remain at my kitchen window
Where I've been feeding them with bread.

British Museum and Senate House
Are solid silhouettes against the afterglow
While in between, the Post Office Tower
Rears its black and phallic length.

Its gleaming glans points upward
To a sparkling slender moon,
To Venus also, brightest of the planets,
Whose light obliterates the lesser stars.

This darkening square is strangely still tonight.
New-roosting birds are singularly mute.
Above the branches of a tall ailanthus tree
A hunting tawny-owl flies silently.

Clerihews on Aphra Behn

Aphra Behn
Was the first woman to live by the pen.
No wonder her biographer
Called her the incomparable Aphra.

Aphra Behn
Is becoming fashionable once again.
What permissive-society-reader can resist her
When she writes of sex between a nobleman and his sister?

Maureen Duffy,
One writer who can never be stuffy,
Claims Aphra Behn's style bears the stamp
Of Firbankian ecclesiastical high camp.

Existentialism

What is existentialism?
These three words were flung
At us from posters
All over Bloomsbury.
Come to Dick Sheppard House
And hear Herbert Read on:
What is existentialism?

The hall was packed, people
Standing against each wall
And sitting in the gangways on the floor,
Seemingly ignored by the speaker
Who read from a script, unable
Or unwilling to project his voice
And never quite communicating.

He spoke for two boring hours.
When he sat down, the Chairman said:
After that stimulating lecture, you will
All be wanting to ask questions
Or will be impatient to take
Part in the discussion, so
Who is going to be first?

There was a terrible silence
Which seemed unending, unbearable.
At last a sudden audible sigh
Of relief as a man stood up
At the back. The question
I want to ask Herbert Read is:
What is existentialism?

Selected Poems

The Tip Wood

A strange sensation I felt there
Waiting in the quiet autumn wood
Sheltered by the man-made mountain
Of blue coal soil and purple slag.

Not that it was just beautiful
To the eyes with the multi-coloured trees
Projected up against the blue-black tip
But it was also the silence and the sounds.

Faint rustling sound of soft fall of leaf
And sudden silence after staccato plop
Of acorn dropping or loose wind-killed twig
On to the dry brittle carpet of the wood.

As though the trees were waiting with me
For the final act, the final definitive act.

Tiddlers

Here where the road now runs to Aberdare,
the old canal lay stagnant in its bed
of reeds and rushes housing dragonflies
which flashed from sunshine into willow shade.

Beneath this very bridge we came to fish
for roach and perch and other smaller fry
like minnows, sticklebacks and tiny frogs
and all these smelt peculiarly of the pit.

A smell of stinkhorn fungus, coal and damp
still clung to them as though they had swum up
some subterranean passage from the mine.

They smelt the house out when we got them home
and, when we changed the water, always died:
clean water killed them.

Cwmpennar

This silent pit,
relinquished by men, has been reclaimed
by nature. There are willows now
in the waste land of the colliery yard;
they shake their shining catkins through
the gutted windows of the lamp room's shell.
The spicy tang of bracken blends
with permanent and pungent smell of coal.
The silver birches huddle closer
and stand like weeping women round the shaft.

All that remains
are two gaunt wheels that cut the line
of hill, the wall-protected shaft,
the pit-head gear in trim, the winding engine
at the ready: for just one man who must
go down each day to drive the pump and deal
with all the mountain water that collects;
its weight would break down the dividing wall
that separates it from Deep Dyffryn,
a pit where men are working day and night.

Deep down below
this yard now overgrown and green,
the pumping station, like an anchored
ship abandoned in the night with all
its crew except the captain gone, remains
an isolated relic dimly lit
surrounded by the water and the dark.
Beneath this tangled wilderness and wood
where boys are playing in the sun,
a man is working under ground, alone.

The Rocking Stone

A stillness everywhere,
The Merthyr mountain bathed in golden light,
I stood above the stile
And waited for the sun to set again.
The Aberaman ponds were pools of blood,
The Brecon Beacons black and jagged lines
Across the afterglow.

The darkness fell before I reached the stone,
A night with navy sky.
I sat against the ruined engine house
And listened to the noises from the town.
Above the mountain murmur of the Ffrwd,
The sadder sound of trucks
And sighing of the ventilator from the pit.

The Tip above Mountain Ash

I stood there on the shining tip, feeling
like flying over the grey slated town.
The air below was a glass bowl, was a clear pool
of Mellte water with magpies for fish, mute
mechanical magpies. As I stood there
above oblique Caegarw I marked again
their long-tailed clockwork flight like black
and white gigantic dragon-flies.

I stood there on the shining tip, hearing
the long Sunday-silence of the day,
hearing it broken again by the harsh morning
call of the vicarage rooks from the Maesydderwen
trees, by the pointless self-pitying cry of the grey
and shabby sheep from the Cefnpennar hill
where the winter sun was stirring the wet bronze
bracken and warming the trodden sheep-paths.

I stood there on the shining tip, staring
at straggling Darranlas across the toy
farm of Gelliddu and the working model
of Deep Dyffryn now silenced for Sunday
soon to be silenced for good and what then
I wondered will become of the lost towns
of Wales dearly beloved and cheaply betrayed
not by exiles only but by home-loving sons.

I stood there on the shining tip, thinking
of the old days of Wales and its people now
(while choirs disband and chapels close, replaced
by drinking club and bingo hall) caring for cars
but having for their language and literature
a cold and calculated indifference.
I looked at the magpies and listened
to the sheep and wondered about Welshmen.

Lark

Helicopter of the hill,
with your vertical take—
off and controlled poise
as you climb, you make
the mountain shrill
with your noise.

Coming in to land,
you drop suddenly
straight as a stone
to meet the ground
but not directly
to your home.

You leave the air
through cold couch-grass
and wind-blown heather
so none knows whether
you merely pass
or live there.

If put to the test
when I was young,
I could find the nest
of any species among
the birds of Wales
except yours.

Colours

The valley's white, white with its tumbling brooks
And pigmy rapids polishing the stone
In frothy streams that slide down slippery rocks
To lose identity in Cynon's flood.

The valley's grey, grey with its threadbare sheep,
Gaunt shabby rams that wait in autumn wood,
Thin haggard ewes that scrounge the winter street
And fragile lambs that freeze in April wind.

The valley's black, black with endemic slag
In tips of ever changing silhouette,
Where, like a funeral, trucks in mourning go
Reflected in the river's tarry shine.

Yet when, in absence, I evoke the scene
The colour of the valley's always green.

Japanese Rice Weed

We could have called it the Welsh rice weed,
Ubiquitous as it is in Wales,
Colouring the coaly banks of all
The black and shining rivers with prolific
Green, sheltering with its foliage the pale
Exotic lilac of the balsam flower,
The deeper purple of the willow herb.

But the pea-shooter plant we named it
As boys, breaking it down with our boots
And cutting our fancied length of tubing
From its bamboo-sectioned stem, which nature
Had already hollowed out and left
The perfect thickness for our ammunition
Of autumn-reddened berries from the thorn.

When we were here last in high summer
It stood broader than a man and higher,
Stood jungle-thick, its elongated smooth
And polished limbs blotched as with blood,
Its heart-shaped leaves hardly distinguishable
From those of its parasite, convolvulus,
Whose frail white bells were tangled in its stem.

Now at this searing end of winter
We see these relics of the last year's crop,
Dwarfed heaps of dead and whitened stalks
Cut down by frost and thrashed by bitter wind;
Yet underneath these dry and brittle sticks
Are curled-up crimson shoots waiting to thrust
Into a straighter and a stronger growth.

We could have called it the Welsh rice weed
For at this time it symbolises Wales
Awakening from its sleep; these virile spikes
Ready to replace the withered stumps, are like
The young emergent Wales preparing to break free
From all the alien clutter of the recent past
To struggle, a new nation, into life.

Craig y Dyffryn

The tips have priority now.
Some are suspect and must be made safe,
Scooped out and levelled by a giant's hand.
They are moving the Craig, more of a wood
Than a tip, covered with birch trees
And almost impenetrable undergrowth.
Harebells grow among the rough grasses
Of its summit and I have seen
A weasel snaking his long body
Through the sheltering brambles at its foot.
Now bumbling yellow bulldozers crawl
And clamber obstinately across the steep
Sides of the tip, blunder through the birches
Like ungainly dinosaurs, lumbering,
Crashing down the trees, tearing giant handfuls
Of the woods, where we picked blackberries
And gathered water cress. All the birds,
From magpie to the long-tailed tit, have gone.
The celandines and wood anemones
Already have been torn up by the roots.
There will be no bluebells this year, no
Branches for the honeysuckle to climb,
No foxgloves in the fullness of the summer.
The tips have priority now.

Requiem

Mourn for the children who in earth are laid
And let us not forget that they were killed
By that sad mountain which their fathers made.

That tip had made tough miners feel afraid
And they, whose darkest fears have been fulfilled,
Mourn for the children who in earth are laid.

The price of coal has finally been paid
With those young bodies violently stilled
By that sad mountain which their fathers made.

Bereaved believing parents, who have prayed
Not to think this an act that God had willed,
Mourn for the children who in earth are laid.

They cannot face the future undismayed
In contemplating all they must rebuild
By that sad mountain which their fathers made.

And workers, who have often been betrayed,
Whose lives again with bitterness are filled,
Mourn for the children who in earth are laid
By that sad mountain which their fathers made.

The Moorhen Pond

This lake was clean (we used to swim in it once)
and so clear that one could see under water
but in the centre it was deep and dark;
legend said it was bottomless, perhaps
an old shaft or a rock-fault common in Wales.

Around the edges there were rushes, reeds
and willows which provided nesting sites;
sometimes we could reach the nests by wading
but had more often to swim out for them.

Since they built the phurnacite plant, things
are different: the willows killed, the coot and moorhen
gone, the water covered with a thick black scum.

But there are fish in it still: red-finned roach
and stickleback, drab and dirty as the pond.

Welsh fish are not fussy.

Christian Unity in Wales

Our chapels all refuse to be united;
A new attempt would cause an awful row
And only make the deacons get excited
So let's keep off that controversy now.

Instead, it would be relatively easy
To join up with the people in the church
As long as we do not become too queasy
At leaving other chapels in the lurch.

We know the church is just the Tory party
At prayer, as someone has so rightly said;
We know their singing's not exactly hearty,
Not coming from the soul but from the head.

Yet we have faults and they must be admitted
Though at the moment I can't think of one.
Perhaps some little sin we have committed,
Some charitable act we've left undone.

But not enough to give them cause to blame us.
Some formula could certainly be found.
And nonconformist tolerance is famous
As once I heard a minister expound,

'To live and let live is the only fair way.
We chapel men regard the church like this:
They only try to worship God in *their* way;
We only try to worship Him in *His*.'

Search Yourself

Admonitory notice search yourself
confronts the collier at the pit head gate
such metaphysical advice
in theologically erudite Wales
search yourself Laertes know thyself
to thine own searched-out self be true
replace Polonius by the psycho-analyst
you on the couch there search yourself
what were you thinking what your motives when
and you young miner crossing the colliery yard
have you searched not only your pockets but your self
your life what doing with it where going when
where whither wherefore and especially why
because why is a psychological question.

Autumn in Wales

Many kinds of metal glisten in the sun,
Copper leaves of beech now lighten to steel,
Now darken to bronze. Pinchbeck necklaces
Of elm sparkle above the chromium
Trunks of silver birch. Gold pieces
Of hazel and sycamore glitter against
The rusted iron of oak and fern or gleam
Between the obstinate summer-green of alder
And elder. Stubborn foxglove leaves still
Linger on the brown loam of the path
Through the bracken.
                    But here the wood
Is windowed by diaphanous old man's beard
Which cannot hide the blood of autumn,
The red, endemic red of autumn, red
Of nightshade, hawthorn, bryony and rose.

Ram

Saddle and shoulders royally marked
with purple dye, rain-clean wind-ruffled
beard flashing white against November gold,
this beautiful lean beast advances
across the cleared-green fenced-in island
in a copper-coloured sea of bracken
to where the still and patient ewes
willingly await their unfamiliar guest.

He holds his fine head high, with its
profile of aristocrat, eyes of dissipated rake,
ears half hidden by the dark eccentric crown
which curls like a shining cast in bronze
of a sculptured pair of giant snails.
Majestically he moves among his dull harem
choosing, discarding; lingers at this one,
half mounts, decides against it and descends.

Suddenly he sees between the barbed wire
an exotic stranger, her back and loins
stained scarlet, marked member of an alien
flock, putting herself forward to meet him.
She stops still as a statue except
for the quiver of her nostrils working like his.
They stand staring in a stupid sexual trance;
now he would jump the barrier if he could.

Just like a man, like every man
since Adam took the apple, like all
our vacillating trapped-in tribe
irresolute before the forked dilemma,
seeking fulfilment where it can't be found,
permanently striving for something else,
creating our own desires, never satisfied,
always wanting the one over the wall.

Colliery Choir

There was singing in the valley in those days, music
From the mines. It was home from the pit, bath by the fire,
Clean white shirt, best suit, grab the copy (tonic
Sol-fah for most of them) and off to the choir.
Curiously effeminate they looked, coal-dust mascara'd
Eyes contrasting with their occupational pallor.

They practised in the most unlikely places:
Upstairs room of a pub, territorials' drill hall,
Boxing club, once the undermanager's office
On the pit-head yard for a part-practice,
Even the first-aid room with all the stretchers
Ranged around the wall, anywhere that was empty.

They never needed a piano. Emlyn's tuning fork
Did the trick. The few times he forgot it
There was always some singer with absolute pitch
Or near enough. 'Give me middle C, Merfyn, will you?
Like cellos now, you basses, head voice not chest.
Feel the sound resounding in your nose. And you tenors,
I want a true falsetto. Sing it sweet, like girls.'

'And remember, next week: the score in your head
Not your head in the score. Eyes on the conductor.
Sorry about that, lads, I can't help my looks.
Don't only watch my hands. My face will tell you
How to sing. And always breathe from the belly.
But don't all breathe together. Stagger your breathing
Or I'll be blown off the bloody rostrum.'

Travelling to local eisteddfodau, they carried
Their black bows in their pockets until ready
To go up on the platform. Often they knew
They had won before they heard the adjudication.
It could be gathered from the comments all around them
After the applause: Duw, there's lovely.
Definite winners, mun. Got it in the bag, ai.

For what we have received

We were not vegetarian from choice
but from necessity; meat cost too much
and allotment salad seemed free.
So there were fragile young
lettuces in season and small
shining globes of radishes,
spring onions which chilled
the throat (jibbons we called them)
and deep purple flesh of beetroot
fleetingly reminding us of meat.

In autumn we finished our meal
with blackberry pudding or wimberry pie,
whichever fruit our eager indigo fingers
had picked that golden day.
My mother had a hand for pastry,
especially for apple tart
made on a large flat dish
and served geometrically neat
with exactly equal slices
making fair shares for all.

In winter we had a thinner time:
sometimes dinner was half a banana
with bread and margarine, though
there was always tea, hot, strong and sweet.
All week we waited for the Sunday joint.
The smell of mint or parsley
can still arouse in me
the excitement we felt
for the small sweet mountain mutton
when it arrived on our table.

Shoulder of lamb with its crisp
brown crust of fat across the top
or breast of lamb, fragrant
with green parsley stuffing
speckled with herbs and chopped
onion, was served with spring greens
and yellow waxy new potatoes
tiny from our own garden.
But the meat was the thing:
we were not vegetarian from choice.

Fox

As I came down from the Merthyr mountain
Through the tunnel of the earth-smelling larches
Into the gold shimmer of the mown hayfield,
Old Brynmor came out of his sheep-pen.

'Got him after all, mun. Look over b'there.
Been keeping us awake all night he has
With his yapping, coming right up on the bank
Close to our windows, disturbing the dogs.
After our pet rabbits he was, I think.
There's no lambs down here now, see.
They are all up the top this weather.
Sometimes I was after him at two o'clock
In the morning with the full moon.
Kept missing him. But I got him today
Just as the light came. Shot the bugger
With this old rifle from thirty yards.
He's over by here. Come and have a look.'

The farmer must have laid him out with care
On the low wall, a magnificent creature,
A big dog-fox, forty-four inches
From nose to tail. He was the colour
Of winter bracken in the sun after frost.
His soft fat brush was brown as the peat
And there was white on legs and throat.

'Many a time, mun, I've shot a rabbit
Through the head at eighty yards. Got to have
The telescopic lens on for that, see.
A rabbit with his brains hanging out
Will still hop about and try to bite you.
You'd think he was bloody dancing, ai.'

The fox looked as if he were asleep.
I stroked the beautiful sleek body
Which was still warm—no, it was the sun.
I could not bear him being dead.

More than anything that glistening morning
I wanted to see him spring off the wall,
Streak across the gold shimmer of the mown hayfield
Through the tunnel of the earth-smelling larches
And gain the freedom of the Merthyr mountain.

'You can have him if you want him
I'd only bury him, mun; take him.
He'll stuff beautiful for show.'

When the Wind
(from the Welsh of Euros Bowen)

When the wind is green,
Seaweed in the sea,
Flesh of the ivy
And window panes of the lake.

When the wind is yellow,
Sand and sea-shells,
Chorus of daffodils
And the moon low in the lake.

When the wind is red
Far out on the sea,
Oats and apples
And fires alight in the lake.

And when the wind is black
And the sun concealed
In the cellars of the lake
I shall find what I have lost.

Collier's Wife

As soon as they had shut the door on him,
They asked her, 'Does he always cough like that?'
She listened, knew at once and answered yes
But felt she had betrayed him when they said
'We'll keep him in for observation then.'
She knew that he would not come home again,
That no one would be there with him at night
To help dispel his fears and fantasies
And nightmares of explosion in the pit,
Of sudden fall of rock, of being trapped
As many in the other valley were.
She knew that she would never have him home
Again nor feel the comfort of his arms,
That this would be the end for both of them.

Horses

One winter morning I was wakened
Not by the customary cold but by horses.
The household cavalry was incongruously there.
Breaking the silence of the Bloomsbury street.
In long line they stretched, at least forty horses
Trotting three abreast: one ridden, two led.

They seemed out of step, beating a confused rhythm,
Their black manes lifting on the breeze like the hair
Of hippies. The brown hock and shank of each horse
Rose from its snowy fetlock like the legs
Of a mini-skirted girl in white boots.
The slender buttocks sensually swayed.

Long after the horses had disappeared
I could still follow their hard hooves
On the tapping surface of the road.
As I listened I seemed to hear the sound
Of different horses, long ago in Wales,
Tougher than these, sturdier, less elegant.

My sister and I would rush out of the house
As we heard them scrambling up the gwli
With a load of coal for the top house.
On these steep gwlis they needed two horses,
The chain-horse doing most of the work, his muscles
Taut as steel, his flanks sticky with sweat.

And other horses which pulled the drams
Across the pit-head yard. These horses all had
Welsh music-hall names like Scrwmpin, Ianto Fullpelt
And Twm Siôn Cati. The hauliers swore
At them affectionately with crude
And obscene words. The horses seemed to like it.

Then there were the huge lumbering shires
Which pulled the council ash-carts; these great
Beasts had won the five-day week long before
The miners. They were sent to the country
Every weekend and boys were allowed to ride
Them to the fields to save paying the men.

Saturday dinner went cold when we heard
The familiar cry: the horses, the horses,
And felt the distant rumble of their hooves.
They formed a longer line than the cavalry
And, for one glorious hour, no soldiers
Were as proud as the boys on their backs.

But I've seen horses running wild and free
Whose ancestors lived on these mountains
Before the Romans came: celtic ponies,
Little horses hidden in the head-high bracken.
I often saw them gallop on the summit
And I knew that they belonged—the real horses.

Autumn in Cardiff

Orange, gold and crimson leaves
fall; and loiter on the wind
like gaudily feathered birds
flying in a slow-motion film.

Reaching a road, I am restrained
by traffic-lights reminding me
that I am merely pedestrian.

But coloured birds continue
to fly out of the trees
and float upon the wind
like lazy falling leaves.

The Last Time

Although I have not climbed
This hill before, I remember
Every detail of it well:
The conflict at the start,
(You thought you had resolved it long ago)
The foreboding on the way up,
(You ought to have replaced your fear by love)
The unaccountable malaise at the top.
I do not want to climb
This hill again.

Although I have not found
This house before, I remember
Every detail of it well:
The brutish guard at the door,
(You have to be signed-in)
The religious maniac on the stair,
(You are required to know the pass-word)
The final and frightening confrontation.
I do not want to find
This house again.

Although I have not seen
This face before, I remember
Every detail of it well:
The fact that it has no ears,
(You have to speak with the sounds in your head)
The realization that it has no tongue
(You try to read the question in the eyes)
The triumphantly malevolent expression.
I do not want to see
This face again.

Ecumenical Catechism

Will those who with the holy roman walk
not drink but only taste the bitter cup,
joined merely in theology of talk,
not act but spend the time in making up?

Will pale horse running riderless away,
whose head was never held by rein nor cord,
distract our listening, when they have their say,
to south bank thinkers who disguise their lord?

Will ruthless light at last on us reveal
the mark of cain before we can atone,
our offering unaccepted, seventh seal
removed to show us what we should have known?

And shall we reap the grain devoutly grown
or gather tares that only we have sown?

Rebirth

Because I have climbed the hill
I have delayed the sunset more than once.
Because I have climbed, the sun
That once had set
Has risen again in splendour
And flooded the mountain
With reflecting auburn light.

So now the hope I may
Delay that other setting,
The greying twilight of the mind,
Revives the thought of what
I'll gain from new ascension.
It will not be vain, I know now
Because I have climbed the hill.

Tree of Heaven

Tall ailanthus trees, like triffids, crowd
more closely round our windows every day.

Already they have killed the fig,
have elbowed out the elm and plane
and stolen all their light.

They press against the wall
and peer into our room
with fustic sorrel face.

We can hear them breathe
and smell their tannic mouths.

At night we hear them coming
to touch our window panes
with green and bony hands
and nervous fingers drumming.

Night in the Square

Orion strides across the sky tonight,
His blue dog, Sirius, tangled in the trees
Which rock with restless movement in the dark,
Their naked branches worried by the wind.
The moon has set, supplanted by the light
Of street lamps picking out the moving branch
With artificial moonlight from the path
Projecting giant fingers on the lawn.

No cars, no people in the square tonight,
Two lovers, only, locked in warm embrace,
Indifferent to the bitter freezing wind
Which shakes the branch and breaks the leafless twig,
Oblivious of Orion and his dog,
His blue dog, Sirius, tangled in the trees.

Allegory

The costume fitted, make-up men
Were working wonders with her face
When I took my decision
Not to begin, not start
The delicate mechanism
Though audience attended,
Actors waited in the wings,
Hostile spectators watched,
The critics ready to pounce.
There'll be no rave notices for me,
Only an angry cast to console
In an empty theatre.
The new production
Will not now take place.

Piéta

The lantern's light projects
two intersecting shadows
from the sombre rafters
on the whitewashed stable wall.
An unmarried mother lies
in an improvised bed,
holding her crying child
in her inexperienced arms.
A man who feels out of place
watches silently from the darkness.
He sees the sweat on her face,
a stain of blood on the straw.
The light flickers again
and the shadows take shape.
Over the manger hangs a cross.

December in the Charing Cross Road

Car tyres hiss through the rain
on the camber of a night-shining road;
puddles change from permissive green
to cautious amber and dangerous red.

I walk along the city pavement, stare
into the branches of a shabby tree,
a plane for several weeks completely bare;
now I am unprepared for what I see.

The leaves have all come back,
ragged silhouettes restless in the night
moved by the wind-swept rain and black
against the cinema's reflected light.

A car back-fires and the leaves scatter
in all directions: starlings chatter.

Rumpelstiltskin

This mountain of straw
To be spun into gold.
Locked in with it now,
There is no getting out.
They all think I can
And only I know
I cannot create gold.

I can make an alloy
But it does not resemble gold.
Perhaps there is something
Wrong with the straw.

Why did I dare
Such a proud promise,
Almost believing it myself?
Only a dearly bought desire for fame?
Or is there a loom latent
Somewhere to weave a miracle?

I brood over the rumpled straw.
The ugly dwarf comes like the face
Of my depression; he does
A partial job of transformation
With glitter enough for a king
But I must pay with money not my own.

Straw into gold
Or gold to straw again
Seems almost easy
Now that I have to spin
A naming of secret names,
The discovery of truth.

Too Soon

The February wind from the east
Had emptied the park of people
In spite of the unaccustomed sun.

The lovers walked beside the ruffled lake
Which lay suddenly as silent as when
A dabchick has dived and disappeared.

There was no sign of spring and the wind
Had made their noses permanently wet,
Their frozen faces ugly with the cold.

Then as they turned before the bridge
They saw them, embroidered on green,
The mauve and yellow crocuses under the trees.

But none of them was open to the sun.
Each one was closed against the bitter cold
As tightly as a sudden angry fist.

When later underneath the darkened trees
He tried to hold her warmly in his arms,
Her obstinate body remained stiff.

Her lips were unrelaxed, her heart
Tight fisted as the stubborn crocuses,
Cold as the February wind.

Youth and Age

when I was
who was me
the tree spoke
the wind sang
when I was
who was me
the wave broke
the bell rang

now I am
who is me
the tree cries
the wind moans
now I am
who is me
the wave dies
the bell tolls